Living With Type 1 Diabetes

Liz's Story

By Elizabeth Mahannah

Living With Type 1 Diabetes -- Liz's Story
Elizabeth Mahannah

ISBN: 979 – 8846003026

Cape Cod Publishing™
2022

Published in the U.S.A.

Cover created by Deb Cubillos

Table of Contents

DEDICATION...5

ACKNOWLEDGMENTS...7

Chapter 1...11

Chapter 2...13

Chapter 3...17

Chapter 4...20

Chapter 5...23

Chapter 6...28

Chapter 7...32

Chapter 8...35

Chapter 9...37

Chapter 10...40

Chapter 11...43

Chapter 12...47

Chapter 13...51

Chapter 14...53

Chapter 15...56

Chapter 16...59

Chapter 17...64

Chapter 18...67

ABOUT THE AUTHOR...69

DEDICATION

I dedicate this book to my husband Jeff, and our daughter Katelyn!

I would not be here if it was not for you!

ACKNOWLEDGMENTS

I want to thank my husband Jeff and our daughter Katelyn for their endless love and support. I would not be here if it was not for you

Thank you to my family and friends!
To Deb and Sharon for helping me with the book and everything to make this happen for me! Thank You

I especially wish to thank my team at Joslin Clinic. Those doctors are

DR.ALYNE RICKER
DR.CINDY PASQUARELLO

Love and gratitude to all my doctors and nurses at Boston Children's Hospital

I almost had to have dialysis if I could not get on the transplant list. Here is the info for the office on Cape Cod and the other clinics and hospitals:

FRESENIUS KIDNEY CARE CAPE COD
241 Willow St.
Yarmouth Port Ma, 026701

JOSLIN DIABETES CENTER
1 Joslin Place
Boston , Ma 02215
617-309-2400

BOSTON CHILDRENS HOSPITAL
300 longwood Ave
Boston , Ma 02215
617-355-6000

SEPTEMBER 1994

Chapter 1

It was the beginning of my ninth-grade year. My new school was called Cape Cod Technical High School. I definitely could not wait to see all of my best friends. I've been waiting all summer to see them and had a burst of excitement. As I started my first day of High School, I was extremely excited!

Things started well at school. I was really starting to fit in for at least the first two months and then things started to fall apart. I was not feeling good a lot. I was getting sick and not being able to come to school. I don't quite remember the day, but I do remember I went into school and all of my friends had asked me where I've been. I told them what had happened to me and that something serious had changed my life and was about to change it forever.

I explained to my friends, '"Well guys let me tell you!" It was a long story, but I explained it pretty decently. I said "a couple of weeks ago, I was not feeling well." I said, "I was really fatigued, thirsty, and urinating a lot."

"Wow that's not good!" My friends said.

"Yes, I was not getting up, sleeping all day long!" I agreed.

My friends then asked, “ What did your mom do to help you?”

Chapter 2

I told them, “Well, she took me to the pediatrician. Dr. K. did some tests. The first test I had to take was a urine test and then prick my finger to get a few drops of blood to test that. The results of the tests showed that I have type 1 diabetes. I had to go right up to Boston Children’s Hospital. My mom drove me up. I was really sick! My blood sugars were 800 and that is not good at all!”

I didn’t even know what was going to happen to me. When I got up to Children’s Hospital, I was nervous and wondered what they were going to do with me. As soon as I arrived, they started an IV right away! I was admitted to the hospital for two weeks. More doctors from a clinic down the street called Joslin Diabetes came over every day to see me and teach me all about Type 1 diabetes.

My friends asked me, "Can other people catch this from one person to the other"? The answer is no. It is in my body, and I began to explain everything about what the doctors taught me. “I have to do this for the rest of my life”, I told them. “The doctors don’t know how I got it. My father was adopted, so maybe someone on his side of the family had diabetes. We knew my brothers and sister did not have diabetes. I am the only one that has this.”

This was definitely a question that was on my mind.

I have to take medicine for the rest of my life to stay alive, because you could die from this disease! I have a whole lot I have to do to take care of myself!

Things I have to do living with diabetes is I have to check my blood sugars with a blood meter. I prick my finger four times a day to get a drop of blood that goes onto a strip in the meter that tells me what my blood sugar count is. I have to do this before each meal and right before bedtime. I also have to be on a special diet and exercise regularly. I have to give myself a needle four times a day as well. That shot is called Insulin that will keep me alive.

My friends asked me, “Do you have to do this the rest of your life”?

“Yes.” I replied.

Chapter 3

It has been a full year now. The beginning of my first year of high school was not so good. Entering my 10th grade year I met with my friends, and told them, “things are not going good”. I explain to them that at 15 years old this is the hardest year of my life. Things are going downhill because I am eating and drinking things I should not, like eating candy, junk food, drinking lots of soda and fruit juice! I didn’t want to measure my blood sugar or take my insulin. My mom would hold me down and give me my insulin. Aside from my diabetes, I had other problems going on. It was so hard on me! I was only 15! The doctors at the Joslin clinic told me that if I don’t take my diabetes seriously and keep it under control, I will be really sick. I could die. That is not good!

I told my friends, “I don’t see it as being a big deal. I am just a teenager. Looking back, now I do!

When I left Nauset High School. I started working at a nursing home in Brewster, Mass. as a waitress. With my diabetes I was getting better and was on top of it the best I could. I was 17 and I wanted to live a normal life.

What is ‘NORMAL’?

Normal is living with a life changing disease. I still don’t know.

Chapter 4

In 2000 a few years later. I started dating this guy named Jeff. Jeff is so supportive, and he knows I have diabetes. He goes with me to my doctor appointments, helping me in any way he can. Even though I have diabetes Jeff loves me. He is my best friend, my partner, my soulmate.
It is a funny story.

Jeff and I met in the Hospital. I was in ICU from a diabetic shock and Jeff was in housekeeping. I was watching Boston Red Sox game when he came over to. see me.

"You are the youngest person up here., he said.

"I am here because I am a diabetic." I told him.

We were talking about the Red Sox till he got into trouble with his boss who asked him what he was doing bothering me. I did not think he was bothering me.

He asked me for my number. I gave it to him.
I did not call him for a couple of weeks because I was scared, but I finally got up the courage and did. We went on our first date and that was the beginning!

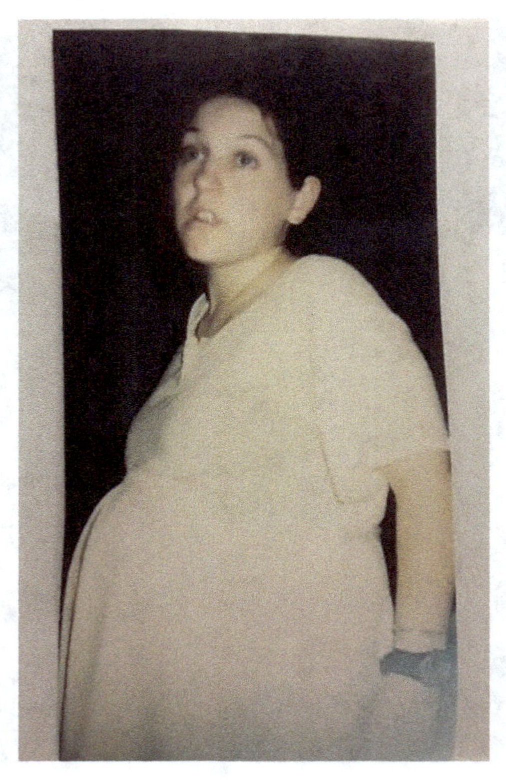

Chapter 5

In 2001 Jeff and I found out I was pregnant. It was very unexpected. I was twelve weeks already and didn't even know I was pregnant till my mom told me. All the times the doctors said I should not have children because of my diabetes. I was still living at home and Jeff was living with a roommate. On October 29th we had our daughter Katelyn Paige Mahannah. 9lbs 1oz

While I was pregnant, I was high risk because of the diabetes. Every week I had to go to the OB/GYN. They would give me a stress test and do ultrasounds. They had to make sure the baby and I were safe. My blood sugars were all great. Everything else was great also!

At 38 weeks my doctors said to come into the hospital, so they could induce me. The baby was growing up to 12 lbs.! Jeff and I went to the hospital that morning at 6:30 am. I got all set up to have the baby. About 9am her heart rate was falling. They sent me in for a c-section.

October 29, 2001. She was born 9lbs 1oz and 21 1/2 Inches long. She was so beautiful! Blue eyes and blond hair. She was born two days before Halloween. We called her our little pumpkin. Katelyn Paige was finally here.

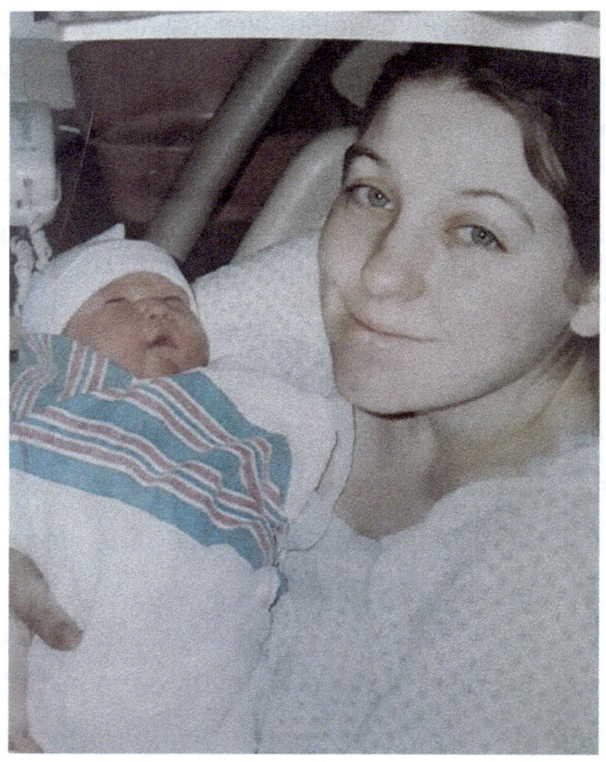

When Katie was born, the doctors had to take her right away. She was having a low blood sugar. They had to feed her right away. While she was inside me, she took all my Insulin. So, she had a low blood sugar.

I had some problems as well. I had to stay a little bit longer in the hospital as well. My blood sugar stared to drop, and I kept passing out and the nurse rushed in to give me dextrose to bring my sugars up really fast through an IV. Dextrose is pure sugar.

I had a lot of stress on my body while I was carrying Katie. Being a type 1 diabetic and being pregnant can be challenging!

FRIDAY, OCTOBER 1, 2010

911: Third-grader praised for calm response to crisis

...er. She remained calm. She gave the location and accurate information. She had everything ready when the rescuers arrived, including locking up the dog and meeting them at the door," he said.

The crisis began early in the morning of Sept. 23, when Katelyn's mother, Elizabeth, 30, of West Yarmouth had an insulin reaction while sleeping.

Mahannah was first diagnosed with Type 1 diabetes, a chronic condition in which the pancreas produces little or no insulin, when she was 14 years old. She carefully watches her diet, and she wears a pump that delivers regular doses of insulin when her body needs it. However, Mahannah is a "brittle" diabetic, someone whose blood sugar can swing from high to low, or low to high, with little or no warning.

In the early hours of Sept. 23, Mahannah's blood sugar level dropped precipitously while she was asleep. By most definitions, a blood sugar below 60 or 70 is considered low. Somewhere in the 50 range, the brain is not getting enough sugar and a person can show symptoms ranging from confusion to drowsiness, changes in behavior, coma and seizure.

Mahannah said she later learned her blood sugar level dropped to 25. And that can be life-threatening.

"I'd checked it before I went to bed. It was fine. I had my regular nighttime snack and made sure I had some juice beside the ...

Katelyn Mahannah, 8, proudly displays a poster her classmates at the Station Avenue Elementary School gave her after she helped save her mom during a medical emergency.

... sweat and going to a seizure.

"I knew what to do because my mother and father had talked to me about it," said Katelyn shyly. "First thing I told myself was 'take a deep breath. Stay calm. Then, call 911. Talk slowly and clearly.'"

... tion they needed. That's important for people to do," Katelyn said solemnly. "You have to stay calm so they can understand you. And if you have a dog, you have to get the dog out of the way of the people who come to help."

Chapter 6

When our daughter Katie was four or five, we taught her what mommy has and what to do if you see mommy acting funny. What diabetes is. We also explained about 911 and what to say. She learned really fast. She knew what to do to get the juice or candy.
Yes, Katie had to call and get those things I needed quite often. I would have very low blood sugars and pass out.

She knew at a young age what to do. I hated to give that responsibility to my child! In a way it was good too to know what to do in an emergency.

When Katie was eight years old in the third grade, the town that we live in, West Yarmouth MA, gave her recognition for saving my life in the State of Massachusetts!

It was the early morning, Katie was sleeping with me. Jeff was working at the hospital overnight shift. I don't remember a lot because I was sick. I was sleeping and I always have a juice by my side. Before I went to bed I had my snack, took my Insulin. I went to bed and all I remember was that I was waking up in ICU on life support. I had a very low blood sugar. It was 20. I went into a diabetic coma. Katelyn looked over and of course she knew what was going on. That I was having a Low Blood Sugar. She called 911, moved our Golden/lab, to the bedroom, moved the coffee table and met the EMTs at the front door.

Yes, she saved my life.

Our town gave her a celebration from the fire department, town hall and her school did so many things for her. She was in the newspaper on Cape Cod and on FOX 25 news. The fire Chief of Mass gave her awards for saving my life!
SHE IS My HERO!
We are so proud of Katelyn for all that, but also for her learning how to help me with diabetes. If Jeff and I did not teach her she would not have known what to do in an emergency.

see MASHPEE, page 10

Third-grader hailed for calm under pressure

Yarmouth girl kept her cool when she had to call 911 during mother's emergency.

By KAREN JEFFREY
kjeffrey@capecodonline.com

SOUTH YARMOUTH – With an aplomb absent in many people far older, Katelyn Mahannah played a vital role last week in saving her mother's life.

And on Oct. 26, in a ceremony at Yarmouth Town Hall, selectmen will recognize the efforts this third-grader from Station Avenue Elementary School took to make sure her mother survived a severe diabetic reaction.

STEVE HEASLIP/CAPE COD TIMES

Katelyn Mahannah knew what to do when her mom went into a diabetic seizure. "When I called, I knew it was important to be calm, not to scream."

Her actions are a blueprint for what others should do when calling 911 in an emergency, Yarmouth Fire Chief Michael Walker said yesterday.

"To say she called 911 at the right time doesn't really cover the situation," Walker said. "She did exactly what people should

see 911, page 10

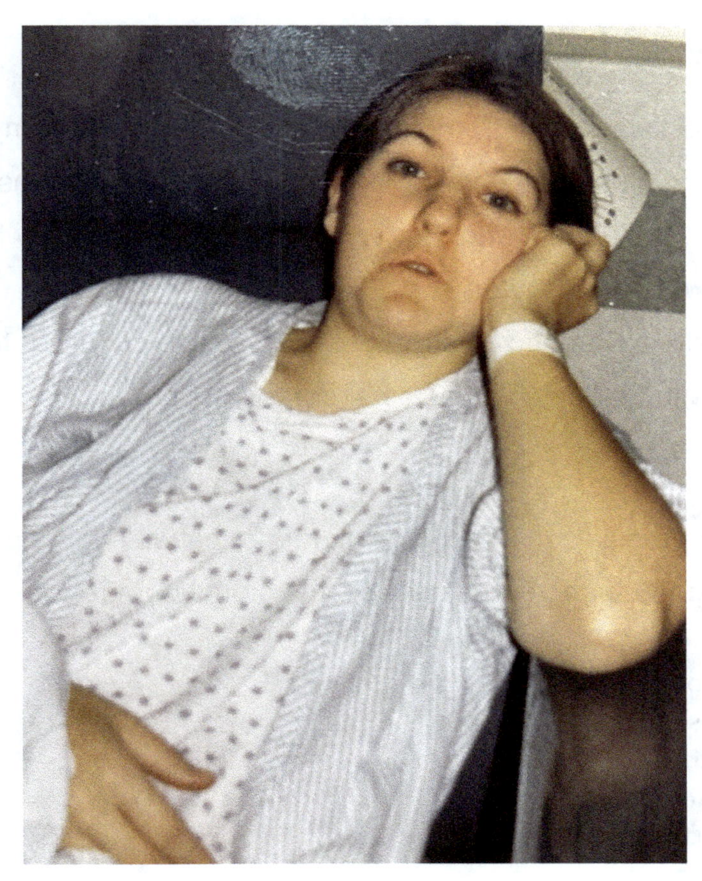

Chapter 7

In 2005 I was having problems with my diabetes with my stomach. I kept throwing up and having bowel problems. I went to the doctor, and they ran tests and I found out what I have with the diabetes.
It is called Diabetic Gastroparesis. This is a condition that affects the stomach muscles and prevents proper stomach emptying.

Gastroparesis can affect digestion. The cause might be damage to a nerve that controls the stomach muscles.

Symptoms
1. Nausea
2. Belching
3. Bloating
4. Heartburn
5. Indigestion
6. Regurgitation
7. Vomiting

I had it so bad for months and months. I could not stop vomiting and having nausea. Not a way I wanted to live life where I was always sick. I did not know when I was going to be sick. It could happen any time. I did not know how to take medication every day for this condition. I will have this for the rest of my life.

Chapter 8

In 2006 I had another condition, this time getting access to my veins. If I was sick and had to get access to my veins, like getting an IV, I couldn't. My veins were so bad.! So, they had to put in a power port.

What is a Power Port?

A Power Port is a special type of port accessible in a single or double lumen, which can withstand higher injection pre-source. A power port must be accessed with a particular type of needle.

I had mine in until 2017.

A power port is inserted into the opening on your chest. The doctor then tunnels the catheter under your skin toward the port at the base of your neck and into your vein. Access the port with a port needle to make sure the port is working properly. The needle is left in place if you need IV therapy within 24-48 hrs. So yes, I really needed this power port because, I was getting so sick all the time.

This with my diabetes was not good at all. I almost did not make it a few times.

1. I was in diabetic comas
2. Passing out, low blood sugars. 0 to 20 range
3. DKA high blood sugars 1010 range
4. Life support- Breathing machine
5. Everything in my body shutting down organs

Not good at all. Really scary. At times the doctors said to me that I don't remember what happens to me when I had low blood sugars. It effects your brain with low blood sugars. Not good at all!

As I look back, all of this is because I did not take my diabetes seriously when I was younger. If I had, these other illnesses would not have happened to me.

I WAS WRONG.

Chapter 9

When Blood Sugar Is Too Low

HYPOGLYCEMIA- Medical word for low blood sugar level. It needs to be treated right away. Why? Because glucose or sugar is the body's main fuel source. That means your body including your brain-needs glucose to work properly.
When blood sugar levels go lower then they're supposed to you can get very sick. Your diabetes team will tell you what your blood sugar level should be and what to do if they get too low.

The causes of low blood sugars levels can happen to kids with diabetes, because of the medications they may have to take. Kids with diabetes may need a hormone called Insulin. This medication helps take the sugar out of the blood and get it into the body's cells, which make the level of sugar in the blood to drop.

Sometimes it's a tricky balancing act, and blood sugar levels can get too low. Kids with diabetes need help to keep their blood sugar levels from getting too high or too low.
Some things that can make low blood sugars

1. Skipping meals and snacks
2. Not eating enough food at meals and snacking
3. Exercising longer or harder than usual without eating something extra
4. Getting too much Insulin

Sign that blood sugar levels are low

1. Feel hungry or have “HUNGER PAINS” in your stomach
2. Feel shaky or like you’re trembling
3. Have a rapid heart rate
4. Feel sweaty or have cold, clammy skin
5. Have pale, gray skin color
6. Have headache
7. Feel moody or cranky
8. Feel sleepy
9. Feel weak
10. Feel dizzy
11. Be unsteady or stagger when walking
12. Have blurred or double vision
13. Feel confused
14. Have seizers
15. Pass out

If you think your blood sugars level could be low, tell someone like a parent, teacher, or whoever is taking care of you.

Chapter 10

How are low blood levels treated?

Eat, drink, or take something that contains sugar that can get into the blood quickly, ask your parents, or who is around so they may give you really sugary foods or drinks, like regular soda, orange juice, cake frosting, glucose tablets or glucose gel. [a tube of sugary gel] Wait about ten minutes to let the sugar work. Recheck the blood sugar to see if the levels are back to normal. Sometimes the bloods sugars can go really low, you might not feel well enough or be awake enough to eat or drink something sugary, which if this happens you would need a shot of glucagon. A hormone that helps get your blood sugar levels back to normal very quickly. Necessary to keep on hand.

I also had no feeling in my feet and hands. It was so bad I had it from my feet all the way to my kneecaps. Treatment can help, but this condition can't be cured.

SYMPTOMS

1. Pain and numbness in the legs, feet, and hands
2. Pins and needles
3. Reduced sensation of touch
4. Uncomfortable tingling and burning

This is called DIABETIC NEUROPATHY

It is a type of nerve damage that can occur with diabetes. The condition most often affect the legs, feet, and hands, which I cannot feel.

I told my family that I cannot feel my feet, legs, and hands. This could not be good! I can step on something sharp, and I would not feel it. It could get worst, possible have my feet amputated.
I could fall down or burn my hands. If I can't feel the water or If I am cooking.

So, yes, this can be really DANGEROUS!
My family could not believe all the things that go along with being diabetic and that you can get really ill with other

diagnoses. That is not good if you don't do what you should and take care of your diabetes.

Chapter 11

In 2010 My fiancé Jeff and I got married. It was a really nice wedding! It was a beautiful day on Cape Cod! A sunny, warm August day for a wedding!

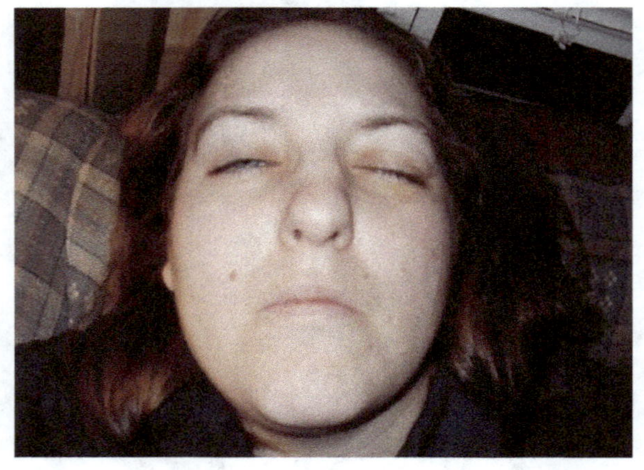

Chapter 12

I am now beginning to get other medical conditions along with being a diabetic. My eyes are getting bad! This is called DIABETIC RETINOPATHY.
It affects the eyes. I had to get needles in my eyes for laser treatment, so I would not lose my vision. To save my eye sight.

What is DIABETIC RETINOPATHY?

People with diabetes can have an eye disease called Diabetic Retinopathy. This is when high blood sugars levels cause damage to blood vessels in the retina.

These blood vessels can swell, and leak or it can stop blood from passing through, sometimes abnormal new blood vessels grow on the retina. All of these changers can steal your vision.

DIABETIC RETINOPATHY symptoms.

1. Seeing an increasing number of floaters.
2. Having blurry vision
3. Having vision that changes sometimes to not clear.
4. Seeing blank or dark areas in your field of vision
5. Having poor night vision
6. Noting colors appear faded or washed out
7. Losing vision

Diabetic Retinopathy sometimes usually affect both eyes

How is Diabetic Retinopathy treated?
Medical control and carefully controlling your blood sugar and blood pressure can stop vision loss.

Medication - one type of medication is called anti-UIGF medication. This helps to reduce swelling of the macula slowing vision loss and perhaps improving vision.
The drug is given by injections shots in the eye. Steroid medicine is another option to reduce macular swelling. This is also given as injections in the eye. Your doctor will recommend how many medication injections you will need over time.

Laser Surgery- Laser surgery might be used to help seal off leaking blood vessels. This can reduce swelling of the retina. Laser surgery can also help shrink blood vessels and prevent them from growing again. Sometimes more than one treatment is needed.

Vitrectomy- If you have advanced PDR your ophthalmologist removes vitreous gel and blood from leaking vessels in the back of your eye. This allows light rays to focus properly on the rection again. Scar tissue also might be removed from the retina.

I tell you, I had to do all of these for my eyes. To keep my sight at one point. I lost vision in both eyes and had to get the Vitrectomy in both eyes. After the other options did not work for me. It was really scary stuff. At one point I did not know if I was going to ever get back my vision. I prayed that I would not lose my vision. This all led back to me not taking care of my diabetes. Trying to be a teenager and having out of control blood sugars.

Chapter 13

Fast forward to 2016. Like I said before I was not doing well. I had an appointment in Falmouth Hospital with Dr. Panagiotis Viagopoulus. He is a NEPHROLOGY doctor.
I went to him, and he did a lot of tests, and it came back I was in stage 5 chronic Kidney Failure. Not doing good at all. Not what I wanted to hear. This diabetes took a toll on me for sure.
I keep looking back on it. I only wish I had taken care of my diabetes seriously. Then I would not have all these health problems.
I have Jeff and our daughter to be with. I am always getting really sick and in the hospital all the time from the diabetes. In my life I could not do a lot of fun things, like take trips, do fun activities. I was always home sick. I am almost 37 years old. I should be doing so much more with Jeff and Katie,
My doctor at Falmouth did the only thing he could do is refer me to Beth Israel Deaconess Transplant Hospital in Boston, for a Kidney and Pancreas Transplant.

Remember my pancreas does not work ever since I got diabetes in 1994. When I was fourteen years old. My pancreas does not make Insulin, that's why I had to give myself four shots a day of Insulin.

So, this is what I had to do. I had an appt at Beth Israel Transplant team. You just can't go in asking and reserving to get a kidney and pancreas. You have to go on a waiting list. They said for just a kidney it can take up for five years to receive one. More for two organs. A kidney and pancreas. I did qualify for the list and my name got on!

Then I had to keep travelling back and forth from Cape Cod to Boston. Two to three hours going up and coming back. Also depending on traffic and the summer when we have tourist season.

Now it is a waiting game to get that call!

Chapter 14

More Information on Diabetes

What is type 1 Diabetes?

Diabetes is a disease that affects how the body uses glucose- A sugar that is the body's main source of fuel. Your body needs glucose to keep running. Here's how it should work.

1. You eat
2. Glucose from the food gets into your bloodstream
3. Your pancreas make a hormone called Insulin
4. Insulin helps the glucose get into the body's cells
5. Your body gets the energy it needs.

The pancreas is a long, flat gland in your belly that helps your body digest food. It also makes Insulin. Insulin is kind of like a key that opens the doors to the cells of the body. It lets the glucose in. Then the glucose can move out of the blood and into the cells.

For someone who had diabetes, the body either can't make insulin or the insulin does not work in the body like it should. The glucose can't get into the cells normally, so the blood sugar levels get too high. Lots of sugar in the blood makes people sick if they don't get treatment

Chapter 15

Type 2 diabetes

Is different from type 1 diabetes. The pancreas still makes insulin, but the insulin doesn't work in the body like it should. The blood sugar levels get too high.

No one knows for sure what causes type 1, but scientists think it has something to do with GENES. Genes are like instructions for how the body should work. They are passed on by parents to our kids.

If your doctors thinks you have type 1 diabetes, you might visit a doctor called a Pediatric Endocrinologist. A doctor who helps kids with diabetes, growth problems and more. The doctor will use a blood test to measure the amount of sugar [glucose] in the body.

How is type 1 diabetes treated?

Kids who have type 1 diabetes have to pay a little more attention to what they eat and do. They need to take Insulin as their doctor prescribed. Eat a healthy balanced diet with accurate CARBOHYDRATE counts.

Check blood sugar levels as prescribed.

Get regular exercise.

Kids with diabetes have to do special things sometimes like eat a snack. Might have to wake up earlier then everyone else. Take their insulin and have some breakfast to keep their blood sugars under control.

What else should I know?

Although this might seem like a lot of work. The good news is that new products and equipment can help. It is easier for kids to take care of their diabetes. Scientists are looking for ways to make it earlier to check blood sugars levels and give insulin. They're also trying to find ways to get insulin into the body without shots and there's hope that one day a cure will be found!

Even though kids with diabetes have to do some special things. It does not keep them from doing the stuff they love. They can still play sports, go out with friends, go on trips, so if you have a friend or someone you know that has diabetes, let them know you can handle it. Being friends is all about having fun

Orange Juice
Bannana
Milk
Sandwich
Milk
Apple
Sandwich
Candy
Candy Bar
Cake
Ice cream

Chapter 16

Keeping track of your blood sugars,

Checking your blood sugar levels is a really important part of taking care of diabetes. Know what those levels are will help you keep your blood sugar under control Something that helps you feel good and keeps you healthy.
Must kids with diabetes check their blood sugar levels before breakfast, lunch, and dinner and then again at bedtime. Some kids need to check more often. You also might need to check your blood sugar doing exercise and when you're sick.

You might wonder why checks are needed in these situationist. Because food, medicine, exercise, and illness all can affect blood sugar levels.

When blood sugar is too high
What is HYPERGLYCEMIA? This is the medical word for high blood sugar level. The hormone Insulin is supported to control the level of glucose in the blood, but someone with diabetes does make enough insulin or the insulin doesn't work property and go too high. Sugar can get into the blood and make the person sick.
If you have high blood sugar levels you may need treatment

to lower your blood sugar. Your diabetes team will tell you what your blood level should be.

The causes of High Blood Sugars

1. Not taking your diabetes medicine when you're supposed to or not taking the right amounts
2. Eating more food than your meal plan allows without adjusting your insulin or diabetes pills.
3. Not getting enough exercise
4. Having an illness, like the flu
5. Taking other kinds of medicines that affect your diabetes.

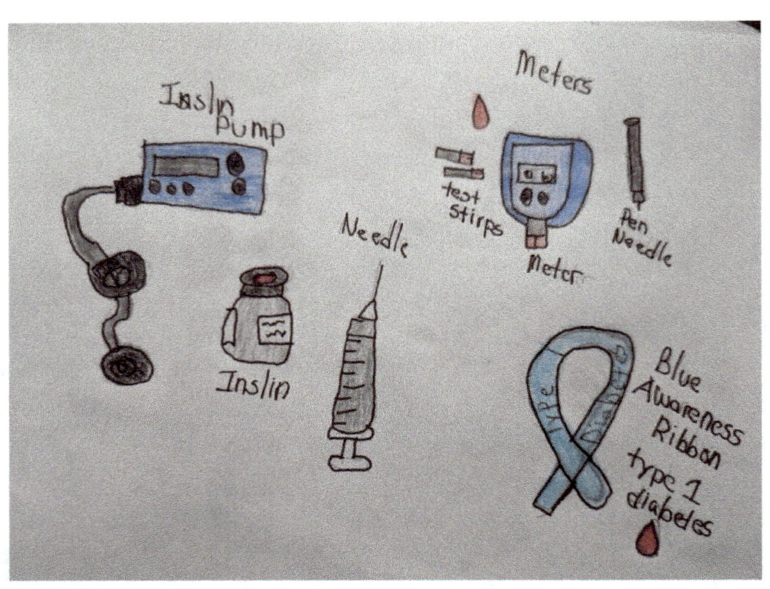
Inslin
Pump
Meters
test
stirps
Pen
Needle
Meter
Needle
Inslin
Blue
Awareness
Ribbon
type 1
diabetes

Signs that blood sugar levels are high

Pee a lot. When blood sugar levels get too high, the kidneys flush out the extra glucose into your urine [Pee] which is why people who have high blood sugars levels need to pee more often and in large amounts.

Drink a lot, because you're losing so much fluid from peeing so much. You can get very thirsty, lose weight. If there isn't enough insulin to help the body use glucose, the body starts to break down your muscle and loss for energy. You feel tired, because the body can't use glucose for energy properly, you may feel really tired.

How can I keep my blood sugar levels under control?

1. Take your insulin or pills when you're supposed to.
2. Follow your meal plan as much as possible
3. Get regular exercise
4. Check your blood sugar level several times a day.
5. Visit your doctor regularly
6. Learn as much as possible about diabetes.

Chapter 17

What is DIABETIC KETOACIDOSIS [DKA]?

Someone who has high blood sugar can develop a serious problem with a name Diabetic Ketoacidosis. This happens if the body gets desperate for a source of fuel. The body wants to use glucose [sugar] but without insulin that glucose stays stuck in the blood and isn't available to the cells, so the body uses fat instead.

But that can sometimes cause problems, because when the body uses fat chemicals, called KETONES. These ketones get into a person's blood and urine and they can make a person very sick. DKA is a very serious problem for people with diabetes, but the good news is that it can be prevented and treated.

Symptoms of DKA

1. You're really tired
2. You're really thirsty or peeing way more than usual
3. You have a very dry mouth

If a person doesn't get treatment?

1. Belly pain
2. Nausea or throwing up
3. Fruity smelling breath
4. Trouble breathing
5. Confusion

How to treat DKA?

GO TO THE HOSPITAL RIGHT AWAY!

Chapter 18

The daily routine

You probably have a routine for checking your blood sugars. You might stick with that plan for a long time, but if something changes, like you get sick, you'll probably have to check more often.
People who use an Insulin Pump or who need to control their blood sugar levels very closely also need to check levels more often. Sometimes you might wake up in the middle of the night to check your blood sugar. They want to make sure your level is not getting to low or high when you're sleeping.

I used to wear an Insulin Pump. It did help a lot in the beginning when it was dropping my sugars to low.
I wanted to tell my story about how I manage my diabetes. Not the way I should have, and I would not have ended up with these other health issue.

Children with diabetes can do this and there is so much support out there and information to learn about.

That was my story!

Thank you!

Liz

ABOUT THE AUTHOR

Elizabeth Mahannah, known to her family and friends as "Liz" was born in Boston and moved with her mother and brother to Cape Cod when she was nine. At 14 years old, she was diagnosed with type 1 diabetes. She was beginning the 9th grade at Cape Cod Tech.

This is her true story of her struggles as she became a teenager and had to deal with a life-threatening condition.

Liz now lives in West Yarmouth with her husband Jeff and her daughter, Katelyn, who at eight years old, saved her mother's life.

RESOURCES

FRESENIUS KIDNEY CARE CAPE COD

241 Willow St.

Yarmouth Port Ma, 026701

JOSLIN DIABETES CENTER

1 Joslin Place

Boston , Ma 02215

617-309-2400

BOSTON CHILDRENS HOSPITAL

300 longwood Ave

Boston , Ma 02215

617-355-6000

Contact Links

Liz can be contacted by e-mail here:
elizabethmahannah@gmail.com

This book is available through Amazon.com. and other internet sites.

Check out Liz Mahannah Author Page on Amazon.com

Watch for Liz's second book coming soon to Amazon.com and other sites.
:

Liz's Second Chance of Life in 2023

www.ingramcontent.com/pod-product-compliance
Lightning Source LLC
LaVergne TN
LVHW020040170826
845678LV00001B/352

9798846003026